Thank You Ruth!

♡ #iamresilient

Jessica Petersen

The Resilience Code

The Resilience Code

How Everyday Systems Run Your Life

JESSICA HANSEN

Published by AmplifyHer

ISBN: 978-0-359-11833-5

First Edition

CONTENTS

INTRODUCTION

Introduction

Can you imagine using a simple tool that could make your life easier? That may sound like a bold promise, but it is the entire purpose of this book. What I am going to show you is how to unlock one of the most powerful tools in your life. This tool will keep you focused, productive and effective even when you are navigating through different challenges.

I know the power of using a resilient system firsthand. Not only because it has kept me focused in times where I could have easily gotten off track. Also, because I teach workshops, coach others and have even worked in corporate positions with the sole purpose of using systems to maximize productivity.

If you are someone who has been looking for a simple way to become more effective with your actions with the ability to stay consistent even when faced with obstacles, you are holding a major solution to becoming more productive and living a resilient life.

What is a system?

A system is simply a list of steps that you're using over and over to complete a certain action. Some people call their personal systems routines.

Routines are systems.

Did you know that even in computer language, systems are written using "sub-routines?! " Not joking. I'm a huge nerd. You can have systems for anything in your life. Even if you're not trying.

So now that you know what a system is, let's touch on another key definition, Resilience.

What is resilience?

Resilience is the ability to bounce back from adverse conditions. **Anything that goes wrong or goes differently than planned is *an adverse condition*.**

For example, as I was driving to the store this morning, I saw a car wreck. For those two vehicle owners, today was a bad day and they were in the middle of adverse conditions. Realistically, they probably will be for a few weeks as they heal any injuries and replace or repair the vehicles.

We will hope and pray that they have a resilient financial system in place in their lives to weather this storm.

So, if we put together these two words, we come up with this idea of a "resilient system."

What is a resilient system?

A system that ALLOWS you to function with ease and flow during adverse situations. The resilient systems you put into your life make everything easier.

A resilient system is the reason that you don't have to get overwhelmed, you don't have to give up! And if you are currently feeling overwhelmed, keep reading, because this book will show you exactly what you need to do.

Resilient systems create the framework for your life.

No matter where you live, or what your occupation is, your life has a basic framework. Some people live in chaos, and their framework is a house of cards. Other people live in ultra-rigid and inflexible concrete structures and their framework topples when there's an earthquake. An actual resilient system is more like a seismic skyscraper that can sway in the wind and roll with the punches. That's what your life should look like! If you're a control freak, lighten up. If you have a glass house, run for cover, because a hail-storm is coming.

Resilient Systems give meaning to the everyday patterns.

You have patterns whether you accept them as such. You probably have a specific order that you wash your body in the shower. A habitual way you drive to your favorite store. I bet you even assemble your sandwiches the same way each time Whether or not you make it yourself or have the sub-shop employee make it for you. These are all systems.

SYSTEMS = ROUTINES = HABITS

This is the base concept you need to understand to make use of this book. Pretty simple, right? See, I knew you would catch on! Systems aren't so scary.

Resilient Systems create constant feedback.

One of the OTHER key concepts that I need you to understand is that a system needs feedback. It is important that you pay attention to your habits and routines. No more mindlessly doing things.

(OK, I heard you groan. I get it.)

I know you can do this small piece. How? Because you already know you want to change something, or you wouldn't be reading this book.

So, fear not, I'll help you learn how to create the feedback loop that you need. Because a system is incomplete without this constant improvement cycle. II will help you to see exactly how Resilient Systems can help you in your everyday life.

We need systems because…

ONE

We need systems because we take too many unfocused actions.

SYSTEMS CREATE FOCUS

Everyone has some built in systems. Remember it's just "the way you do a thing." Systems are not just for computers, in fact, the entire computer logic was created because people had systems, a group of repeating tasks they did over and over, which the computer could do for them to make it happen faster and more accurately.

Think about things you do around the house, how you wash your dishes, put away your groceries, fold your clothes, etc. These are examples of systems you have in your life that aren't on the computer. You can even look deeper, and realize that for your laundry system, you have a few sub-systems - a different one for shirts, socks, pants, and underwear. Each small routine you have goes into the big picture with the others. They all have a very micro-specific goal they're accomplishing.

This is the key. Always keep in mind what you're trying to accomplish - systems create a focused set of actions.

Another system you can have in your house that isn't a computer system, is a list of optional tasks based on the situation. For example, when my kids want to play video games, they must complete a specific list of tasks before they're allowed to play.

Now, if they already brushed their teeth, they don't have to do that task again. But they have the complete list to reference. The goal of this system was to end the interruptions. They don't have to keep asking over and over if they can play. Systems create focus for me, even though I am not doing the tasks for myself. I can now take my time and do another set of tasks with it.

Systems saved my sanity - allowing a focused mind! I created this (not so fancy) laundry system. I have 4 kids. 4 kids and 2 parents make a lot of laundry. And, being Type A, piles of laundry don't work for me. I often work from home, so I have to look at it all day.

Hanging out in the corner, giving me the stink-eye all day. I also live in the forest, where we have a septic system, not on city water/sewer.

If you've ever lived on a septic system, you know you have to baby them sometimes, and respect that if you do things wrong, you're literally up shit's creek. That means, you can't save up your laundry all for one day and marathon through it.

It stresses the septic and can cause a host of messy issues I don't want to go into here. So, I developed a simple system for my family. Remember, a "system" doesn't always mean computers! Two loads per day, starting on Monday, every day, until it's all done.

The top 2 reasons why businesses fail are bad management and financial - solid systems can solve both.

Bad management isn't usually because of bad people - it's usually inefficient systems, and a poor decision-making process. For example, When I worked in a corporate job, I experienced good management and poor management - either directly or indirectly. Some of it is on HR, because they made decisions to hire (or promote) people that were difficult to work with - causing lots of turnover, and constant training and retraining, which makes the department output suffer. Some of it was coming from the top - having departments with conflicting goals - caused a ton of contention and prevented optimal solutions to problems because ultimately employee performance reviews were based on the specific department's goals, not the company as a whole. You run a company into the ground if this conflict is too great.

Decision trees are a way solve the poor decision process. What's a decision tree? It's just a matrix showing how to make a particular decision. Especially a complex decision.

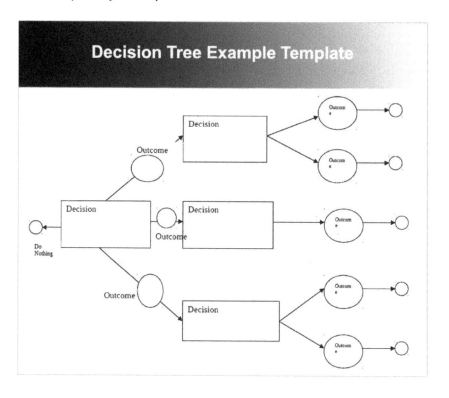

There is no substitute for having a solid logic to a plan. Yes, I am left-brained, and I adore a well-laid out flow chart! If you have a good logic in place, decisions become easier to make. For example, a budget. When you have an unexpected expense come up, and you don't have the emergency fund complete, the money has to come from somewhere. In the instant you can use a credit card, but you still have to pay it back!

You have to look at the budget and decide which item you're going to pull from for the month/quarter/year. There is definitely some room for following your intuition instinct here. But if you have the budget in front of you, it's much easier to see plainly which options you have to choose from.

Financial mis-management

Not having a solid strategy for what to do when you make sales in your business can be detrimental. Super common with MLM moms - they make a sale and pocket the cash. Next time they head to the store, they use that cash to make their personal purchase. Mixing business and personal finance is one of the fastest ways to crash your business.

Over-investing in inventory is another reason financial mis-management is cited. How does it happen? Business owners sometimes don't study the market demands. You have to have a systematic review before you invest.

Misalignment with goals

What prize did you win this month? Did you actually sell the inventory you needed to make your activity level in sales, or did you buy it yourself to keep your upline off your back?

You don't have stress because you have built in a routine for getting all of the core functions done in a manageable way. Your business systems create a more relaxed and tension-free office.

You can use the prioritization system you have because you know what your focused goals are. Simply by evaluating each item on your list against your core goal(s) will tell you if it's something you need to do now or add to the parking lot. Wait, you don't have a parking lot for your ideas and things to do later items? Don't have a prioritization list? *See the Time Freedom Formula Download at www.TheJessicaHansen.com*

Think back to the laundry example I told you about. Because this system is running all the time, it's never building up to become overwhelming. Same with the other chores around the house. Or your finances. Or you customer follow up.

Now, because you have a solid system, you can delegate the rest of the "stuff." Writing down your process/system keeps you from having to spend so much time training someone to do the work.

For example, my chore charts included a list of each task sorted by room so there was never a question of what had to be done in order to have the chores completed. Boy I sound like a dictator! It gets the job done.

Another example of this is the babysitter binder I wrote when I went on vacation the first time after my daughter was born. It's a two-inch binder, with divided sections detailing exactly how to run everything in the house and everyone's approximate schedules, likes/dislikes, even the dog's known vocabulary was written down for reference. At which point I learned that he knows almost 50 words!

I created it when my kids were toddlers for my mother in law to come and watch my kids. This system made it much easier to have time away without feeling the overwhelm of leaving my babysitter ill equipped.

So, what makes a system a system? A Constant feedback loop and documentation. Ask yourself: What are the results that I want? Now ask if you're actually getting the results. To be an actual system it *must* have a closed loop.

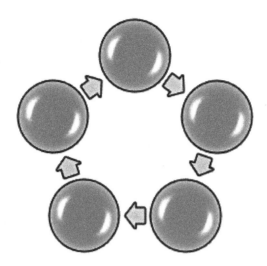

This is the missing piece in most people's systems and routines, because when you don't do it the same way every time, it is not a system.

You can't know if something works if you never do the same thing. This is the importance of documenting the system. It doesn't have to be a complicated flowchart. Most of the time, a piece of paper with a bulleted list (or a list scribbled on a napkin) will work. As long as you're keeping track of the paper!

There are some amazing phone applications that work for this, but let's not get too complicated here. We're using the KISS method. By the simple act of writing down what you're doing, you can come back to the list and know right away if you're doing the task the same way the next time or not.

You have to decide up front how long you're going before you have a review. Note your ideas for changes as you go, but don't make changes until you hit your time-interval's end. Otherwise you're back where you started with no system in place, because you didn't repeat the system. For example, think about putting your clean clothes away. You put them in the same place (ok, ok, at least the same drawer...) so you know where to look for them the next time you want the item.

Do you have kids? How many times can't they find a special toy because it's never left in the same place?!

If it was never in the same place because you didn't have a certain drawer, you'd be wasting time looking every time you wanted to wear it.

Resilient systems create a safety net...

TWO

Resilient systems create the safety net for your life/business

SYSTEMS ARE LIKE INSURANCE

If you have ever experienced something unexpected and did not have insurance to protect yourself, you know how important it is. Insurance is there for catastrophic events. You almost never have to use it. But oh boy are you sorry when you don't have it in place before the disaster strikes. Being in a car wreck without comprehensive insurance, and not getting anything to replace the vehicle is an example of this. Once I wrecked my car when I was a pizza delivery driver. Talk about making it difficult to do your job. Luckily, I did have full-coverage insurance and a week later my car was drivable again, so I could get back to work.

Systems are like insurance for your time. There's no other foolproof way that you can prepare yourself to use the time the wisest way possible. Unfortunately, systems and insurance are both often overlooked, or underutilized.

Fear keeps us from acknowledging that we have an issue sometimes, therefore we avoid coming up with systems and true routines. It might be the fear of losing out on having fun. Or the fear of inflexibility. Or even (*shudder*) the fear of systems being too hard to create. Newsflash, these are all false. There is nothing scary about systems and routines, it's all in your head.

Overwhelming things tend to be avoided, and solving these issues requires facing big things that can seem too big. Breaking things into smaller pieces solve the problem. Maybe you've heard of eating an elephant? Sometimes the simplest things are the answer. Have you ever been doing something fairly complicated, like cooking barbeque sauce from scratch? You spend all this time cutting the vegetables into small pieces, and then put it all into a pan to cook it down into a smooth
sauce. The second time you make it, maybe you grab the food processor and save yourself hours of time by mincing everything at the beginning instead of chopping it, because your friend mentioned that's the way she does it. Then you think to yourself, "why didn't I think of that?" That kitchen aid sitting on your counter isn't there for decoration after all...

Along with being a safety net, you get to relax more.

Systems create a place of Less stress because you'll have a cushion of cash/ resources and time. How does that work? Think about those automatic savings plans you see banks advertise. If you've never seen an ad, google it, the premise is that there is an automatic transfer from your checking account to a savings account at a steady interval of time, monthly or weekly. Having a routine savings plan so you have an emergency fund when the car dies. I remember having to borrow money when my van died. I was a single mom with two kids, looking at $1800 in car repairs while my vehicle sat undriveable at the dealership. I didn't have stashed resources available to me, and I didn't have a car to get to work. That's up a creek.

Building in some downtime into your schedule is another easy system you can implement so you can cover anything that runs over during the week. I generally don't schedule things on Saturdays because I catch myself up then. Why then? My schedule allows me to be home with my family, so I don't have running around to do, no one to drop at school, and no client work. Alternatively, you can have a random day where you JUST catch up. I talk about this in the to-do list download.

You can have a shopping system too, building up the food in your pantry saving you time and money easily every week. One simple example is to buy two of the kids' favorite boxes of cereal instead of one to save yourself a trip to the store when you run out too quickly and your picky son refuses to eat anything except Kix (true story.) My second son only ate Kix for months as a toddler.

Having solid systems in your home/business will also allow you to take time off without worrying about how to cover yourself. You know what needs to be done so you can do things ahead of time. Something as simple as scheduling social media posts, emails etc. can save you a lot of time. Even meal prep for your family so they don't starve while you're not there cooking for them every day because you're traveling for a business conference.

You're able to delegate with confidence because you have everything written down. This goes back to examples like the babysitter binder. Because your home is systematic/routine, not everything piles up for you when you get back, because everything is under control when you left. Sorry, laundry will still pile because of what's in your suitcase. But I promise it will be manageable.

Systems can create extra income

Passive income can generate automatically for you when you have a solid system running, even when you're not. Your website is still running collecting leads. Your digital products auto-deliver to your clients when they purchase if you have them set up right. You have your clients on auto-ship when your business deals with physical inventory. Your emails are all scheduled ahead of time to go out and maintain your client and potential client relationships. And, you're scheduling your social media marketing ahead of time and not missing the key posting times.

All of these small micro-systems fit together into your overall business and home strategies like puzzle pieces.

You will progress faster in your business…

THREE

You will progress faster in your business if you have solid systems.

There's one goal that all women and men have when they go into business - to GROW THAT BUSINESS. It's either growing for impact or growing for money. Dig deep, it will always come down to one of these two reasons. I'm not judging which is better or worse, just stating a fact here. One of the fastest ways to grow your business is to create a repeatable and scalable system to grow it.

Strategic growth

Creating business goals and systems for accomplishing them, as well as reviewing the outcomes. A strategy is all about making choices when you have many opportunities in front of you. A CLEAR strategy will give you direction for each choice to make sure that you're following your path that you set. By having a system of overall business goals on an interval review - so you're always coming back to them - is critical if you want to grow strategically.

It's easy to start a business, but it's hard to keep it going without a strategy for using your time and money wisely!' If you're just tossing money and resources at every opportunity that presents itself, you're not being strategic, and you're wasting your money. By creating the goal review process, you'll always be prompted to come back to the goals to make sure the opportunity is aligned with where you want to go.

More focus on the core goals

By having a core system of your goals and the review of those goals, you know what you should be spending resources working on and how to prioritize all the things. If you're struggling with your time, find a strategy to take things off of your plate, and make sure you're focused on the main goals' activities. Did you download the Time Freedom Formula yet? You can get it at www.TheJessicaHansen.com.

This is one rock-solid method to use your time most effectively. This is how I was able to be a single mom while working a full-time job, having two kids in school, sport, and scouts, and still have the time and energy left to finish my bachelor's degree. I had to count every minute. This works in your business too. Probably even better because you don't have kids interrupting you when you're working at the office!

More Time

For those things you can, delegate or eliminate the things on your list that are not your top priorities. You'll find that most things can simply be eliminated, without a huge impact, though you will definitely feel better! Many things you can't eliminate can be delegated to others on your staff, and sometimes even delegated to the computer so you'll never have to think on them again.

If you find that you're easily distracted, make a list of distractions to eliminate in your life. ANYTHING can be a distraction if it's not directly related to the goal you're working toward. Even good things, like reading books or spending time on learning new productivity applications on your smartphone. If you're not headed toward your goal, then you're distracted by something. Write down what you're doing when you realize that you've gone astray, and make sure you're aware of it next time so you don't repeat the mistake. Oh, you're human? Yep, maybe on the third or fourth time you can eliminate it.

You've already removed the wasted space in your calendar, (See the Pristine Time Management e-book/system at www.TheJessicaHansen.com), so now you can get down to business by making sure you're scheduling yourself specific times to do specific tasks. And DOING them. Not waiting. Not procrastinating. Not doing something, or one last thing first. Just go do the task you have scheduled. Because you've likely over-allocated the time for that task that you're doing, use the rest of the time block to work on something else or reward yourself for doing the thing.

Grouping like or similar activities will actually save you a lot of time during your day as well. I learned this lesson about running daily errands. I live 5 miles out of town. That's roughly a 10-minute drive one way, and rarely is less than a full hour per trip. I found that by combining the different errands I needed to run, consciously thinking about where I needed to go ahead of time, I was able to get WAY more errands done in that hour. Strategically planning your route (think about all of the delivery drivers!) can save even more time since you don't have to drive back and forth. The simple system of combining trips into town saves time, gas, and sanity.

Less wasted money

Let's face it, less manual labor means freed up resources. You don't have to pay an assistant to do the work if you automate it. There are literally hundreds of ways to automate work using software and workflows, and you really don't have much of an excuse not to automate the things you can.

For those things you can't automate, delegate them. Your time is worth money. Is your time worth more per hour than your assistant's? How about your kids? They can help do things too and are often more capable than we give credit for.

One of my favorite delegations for the moment is using the click-list at the grocery store and letting them do the shopping, instead of wandering the aisles and impulse buying. Plus, no crying monkeys hanging off the cart knocking boxes off of the shelves as you go down the aisle. Yep, had that happen. I do have 4 kids. By putting my order in on the website, I can add things from my list, and when I look at my meal plan, often I can skip the step of even making the grocery list too. Bonus time savings! And, I can make sure to use the digital coupons and special offers they have available without having to pick up the ad at the door to see what's on sale.

After work, when you're picking up the kids from school or daycare, the Simple trick of keeping a box of snacks in the car keeps you from having to drive-thru for lunch or dinner, because they can hold-off until you get home. The system here is in keeping it stocked without running out! See how simple the system can be?!

Systems give you more creativity

Having solid systems in place gives you sanity, and When you're not stressed, your brain juice flows more freely. You're not having to worry about what you didn't finish, or when you'll get another thing done. Did you know Stress hormones cause brain function to switch to fight-or-flight, not critical thinking? Having the fight-or-flight mechanism activated is not using your brain to its fullest potential, so you're not able to create anything.

When you have time to meditate, because you've added it into your schedule, you get to receive the inspiration. This is so important. Your inspiration doesn't have to only be in the shower because that's the only down time you allow yourself daily! Seriously, the shower is one of my most common places to receive the biggest inspiration downloads. I hear the same thing from others. Interesting, right?

Also, when driving, drive in silence. I get a lot of ideas there too! Voice recorder is pretty handy and legal! Your brain is engaged in the driving, and you can let your subconscious mind churn while you're on the highway. It's amazing how refreshed you feel after the silence too.

Another trick is that If you find, because you're now becoming aware of this kind of thing, that you're more creative at a certain time of day, you can now schedule yourself some "downtime" at that particular time to just be and invite the inspiration because you have everything else you have to do already accounted for.

There are so many benefits to systems in your business! Money, time, revenue, creativity, and other resources just aren't going to be as used up when you're working smart! You'll be growing your business on autopilot because you are just hitting your goals without trying too hard and burning yourself out.

Systems create more peace

FOUR

Systems create more peace.

Crazy things always happen, but you can have a no stress attitude knowing you can deal with it.

You can't avoid all situations, no matter how hard you try. There's always going to be something unexpected happening to you or around you. But here's the thing. When you have solid systems in place, you don't have to stress about any crazy happenings. Why don't you have the stress? Because you don't have to think about what you need to do when you have solid systems. You can run them without thinking because they're automatic and written down.

One time I actually had to leave my corporate job to pick my son up for joking that he was going to blow up the school. I honestly can't make this stuff up. Boy did that throw a wrench into my plans for a week. Not only did I have to pick him up from school that day, he had out of school suspension for the following three days. If I didn't have a solid plan for working my job from home, I would have left my team out in the rain. Another chaotic time I suddenly became homeless with a toddler. I had a list in my head of what I needed to do because I took my responsibility as a mom really seriously. We needed shelter, food, and diapers. After that was covered, we could sit and figure out a longer-term strategy. Getting yourself clear on the ACTUAL problems without all of the emotional baggage can really set you up for success in a crazy situation. Having a prioritization process really does matter. Even at age 19…!

Another small emergency plan we have at our house, is having a written list for what to do when the power goes out, how to plug in the corded phone, turn on the generator, and how to hook it up to the house. Since we live in the country, literally a mile from the end of the power line, which arrives at our house from the other side of the forested coastal mountain range, we often lose power during snow and windstorms.

Do things automatically to continue on when your head's a mess.

When you can't even process what's going on around you, you'll be so glad your chore charts are keeping your kids on track, so your house isn't a disaster too. There is actually a lot of comfort in directed and routine manual labor. Keeping your hands busy with the systems you have for getting things done will keep you from sinking into the emotions of chaotic times.

If you find yourself in a rough patch where you are forgetting to do things, automatic bill payments and direct deposit of your paycheck keep you from having to physically remember to pay your bills through the stressful time, saving you potential late fees. Things feel so much worse when you're missing payments - no one wants those notices. These small systems will keep you on top of everything.

Making sure every one of your appointments are in your calendar will keep you from not showing up when you need to be somewhere, because you have them set up to remind you based on the approximate drive time to get to the destination. Make yourself a system to add the appointments right to your calendar as you make them, not writing them on a gum wrapper, or an old receipt. In the best-case scenario, you add it directly to your smart phone calendar while you're still on the phone with the receptionist.

Create built in space for your problem solving.

With regular review intervals, you're creating space to solve the problems you're having with your routines, systems, and processes. You'll begin to recognize what pieces are out of alignment for you, because you are Reviewing what's on your goal list, your current systems, what the meaning of life is for you. If you want to grow yourself and your business, these are critical reviews. When you build them in automatically, you are miles ahead because you no longer have to remember to remind yourself to do the reviews.

Sometimes, I find that I'm extremely irritable and distracted. Everything seems to be piled up on me, and I lose all motivation. To fix this, I'll take what I call a "Reboot day," and I'll stop all work on what I "need" to work on and do whatever feels like the biggest burden. This is one of my best tips for managing life when it's feeling heavy. I find that once I do the ONE thing I've been putting off, I'm able to bust through the rest of my list at lightning speed. I don't know why it works, but I promise it does. For more of my tricks, you can download my top ten ways to tame your massive to do list.

Brain-dumps and writing EVERYTHING down are a few more things I use routinely. Get the clutter out of your head! If you can create the space in your mind, you'll feel so much better about the things you're physically doing. Your brain can sift through all of the problems you're solving at the moment in the background, and you won't have to worry about forgetting anything because you already wrote it down.

More time because you don't have things left undone.

When you have a solid system in place, you'll stop having things stack up on you. The everyday chores are smaller because they're all on rotation at home. Same thing in the office. If you're constantly keeping your emails under control, you're not falling behind, and it takes less time every day to achieve the goal of inbox zero. (Do you know how liberating it is to actually have inbox zero?)

Don't forget that you can schedule longer-term tasks for yourself. You'll never have to wonder when the last time you changed the furnace filter was, or when it's time to fertilize the lawn. It's all in your calendar. And because you're reviewing your calendar weekly, you're ahead of the game in time to head out to buy the filter or two, so you never run out of them entirely!

Next time your Mother-in-law calls and says she's stopping by, there's no "hurry up and scramble to clean up because someone is on their way over" happening, because you've got it all under control, and you're not flustered when they arrive. You can enjoy the visit with your extended family without the feelings of being judged, hoping they don't open the closet or look under the bed. You might even have time enough to make a pitcher of lemonade and a snack to greet them with. Won't that be impressive?

It's easy to delegate once you've documented.

One of the principles of good systems and routines is that you have them all documented. Again, this doesn't have to be elaborate. A simple list of tasks in the order you do them is sufficient. This is so helpful when you're asking someone to do something for you while you're not available because you are on the beach in a tropical location, of course!

Remember, kids can do so much more than we think. When my second son was 6, he was doing his own laundry with a stool because he wasn't tall enough to reach into the top-loader and get the clothes back out! Of course, you may end up spending slightly more on laundry soap because it seems to run out a little faster when you have the youngsters using it. If a little is good, a lot must be better, right?

I think I've mentioned before about our video game list, it's so plain and clear what the expectation is, there are no questions, interrupting, or bugging. It has picture icons for the non-readers, and word descriptions for the older ones. There is no debate. All I have to ask is "will I be happy with it if I go check?"

And oh, the grocery store! Make sure you have someone else do your shopping - all you have to do is create the list online, and they shop, bag it, and load it for you! Of course, you have a meal plan in place to make your list from, right? (See the Glowing Nutrition e-book available on my website www.TheJessicaHansen.com.) Don't waste time browsing and window shopping, you'll be spending more than you wanted, and adding more things to dust in your living room. I'm sure that rose-gold camel figurine needed to come home with me though. He looked so lonely on the shelf.

Your personal growth comes easier.

When you make your personal growth into a routine, it happens naturally. You don't have to consciously choose a time to read the book that's been collecting dust on your nightstand, and your podcasts are loaded on your phone to listen to while you're driving. You won't be half-consuming the content, so you can actually implement thing things you're learning about in your studies. You're not going to feel flustered and like change is a burden.

You can travel to workshops and conferences without worrying about things at home going awry, or constantly testing to check up on everyone to keep them going. There are clear instructions left behind for caring for your home and pets, and the kids have no way to argue with the babysitter, because you detailed their routines as well.

All of these systems seem like they would be a burden to set up, but once you face that fear head on, your life will become more peaceful. You'll have space for the things you need to do, and energy to create the things you love around you.

Misconceptions

FIVE

Misconceptions

Misconception #1 : "Systems are too restrictive."

Wrong. Systems actually create more space for you to create solutions for the problems you're facing. But how is that possible? I know that's what you were going to ask me next. Here's the thing. The systems and routines you have are a framework for your life, business, work, whatever you're doing. Remember? It's just a set of habits. Think about some of the habits you already have going on.

Do you have to think about how you're driving to the grocery store?

Oh, you don't?

See?

You have a mental system already in place that you're referencing without thinking about the directions or where you have to turn next. While you're driving, you're actively thinking about other things. Or you're singing along to the radio... I know, we aren't all always thinking in silence. You actually created that mental space to think about something or DO something else while you executed the system.

I mean, sure, you had to think about where you were turning the first few times you drove there, but then it became a pattern for you, and you're simply following along with it. This is the beauty of systems. You can create this space in so much of your day that you're wasting right now.

You don't have to create such a detailed routine that you're scheduled down to the minute, so I don't want you to be confused by that either. You need to create smaller systems and leave space in between for those things that come up. This is one reason you'll find comfort in creating a morning routine and an evening routine, and then leaving some space in between. If your morning routine is more than an hour or two, I leave that as two just in case you include showering and exercise in your routine, it's probably over-full and will feel burdensome after a short time.

If you're not sure how to create a morning and evening routine, check out my Pristine Time Management e-book. There's a worksheet you can print out, as well as a detailed explanation of how to use it for maximum efficiency.

Misconception #2: *"Systems have to be on a computer or involve software."*

Wrong again! Ha! I fooled you. Sure, systems and routines are faster when you can automate them, meaning have the computer do them for you, but there are plenty of things you can do as a system that has nothing to do with a computer.

I suggest automating and programming tasks to happen with software only in places in your life or business where it makes sense. In fact, if you took my time-personality quiz, you may have received a result that actually steers you away from automating a lot of your productivity and to-do. (Did you miss that? Take it here: http:thejess.link/quiz)

Computers and software were originally designed to make life easier or process things faster. Now, they often end up complicating things because we have too many different software and applications running. Take a step back, and evaluate all of the systems you have, and don't just download a free app for the heck of it. Take the time to decide if there is a value in it. If you do download it and find that it's not fitting your needs, delete it. Don't let it clutter your phone, computer, or life!

Misconception #3 "Systems are too hard."

Oh boy, I thought you were going to get that one right. This is also a false statement. Remember how I talked about systems being habits? You're naturally creating systems all the time. What you're doing wrong though, is recreating them each time you go to do something. Trust me. Stop and write down what you're doing next time and see if you can come back and repeat what you did to accomplish a certain task. What you'll find is that it took you less time because you didn't have to remember what you did or think of some new way to do it.

Recognizing that you already have a system of habits and routines is fundamental to accepting the idea of implementing new systems into your life. I know you're stubbornly arguing with me that you don't have routines. But I'd invite you to take a second look. Go back and think about driving to a frequent destination. You likely take a shower with all the soaps in order too. Take this first step and accept that you're already doing things out of habit so focus on that thing you're already doing.

You're not going to be adding in new systems to your life until you get the ones you're already doing under control, so you don't need to get ahead of yourself in thinking that either. When you start feeling that something you're creating a system for is difficult, take a break. Let your subconscious ponder it while you go do something else. And if you're having a really hard time coming up with a way to do something, Google search is going to be your friend.

I don't think using someone else's system as a base for doing your own is a bad thing. I'm not advocating doing EXACTLY what someone else is doing although, following a recipe could be considered a copy of someone's system... but let's not get hung up on semantics. I rarely suggest a carbon copy of someone else's system, because very few people have identical needs for any one system. So, use the search results as inspiration, and create your own system from them.

Misconception #4: "It takes too long to create systems."

But will it take you months to create a perfect system? No! Unless the process or system is something that you're rarely actually doing, a couple of weeks should have all the bugs killed did you know that computer program errors are called bugs? That's what I'm referring to here. If you're following my previous instructions of writing things down, and using your instructions, then reviewing the results to improve the system, then you will be running with expert systems quickly.

Again, if you're getting bogged down in the details and things start feeling overwhelming, take a short break, change your surroundings, and then come back to it. If that fails, Google it. I know you're just looking for an excuse if you still haven't finished it after you've searched for inspiration.

Resilience happens

SIX

Resilience happens in 5 areas of life

If you've been following along until now, you can probably guess that my ideals on systematizing your business surround running as much as you can on autopilot. There are a few reasons for this, you don't have to do as much manual labor, things happen faster because there aren't papers or tasks changing hands, and you don't have to pay someone to get these things done. And, yes, I realize there are a lot of things you can't take the human out of, but let's talk about a few that you can.

Business

Scheduling systems are a HUGE time and money saver. The main argument for them is that there isn't any back and forth discussion about when people can schedule time with you. And, even better, once people do schedule time with you, you can have appointment reminders automatically sent to them at whatever intervals you want, via whatever medium you want, most commonly email and text. Because you've automatically set up your scheduler to remind them, you don't have to remember to remind them. Huge win.

But what if someone you don't want to meet with schedules time with you? Don't worry, you can even automate the screening process using forms, and if they still get through, you can always cancel the appointment from your end. Remember, we've talked about this before - just because it's systematized and documented doesn't mean it's set in stone.

Next, let's talk about email auto-responders. If you're connecting with many people at all, this is going to help you with your relationship maintenance. Set up a series of emails for your audience to receive over a period of time. I'm not going to suggest this timeframe, because the market changes, and I don't want to steer you astray, and they will get to know you and your business slowly. This isn't just for online businesses. ALL businesses should be in contact with their current and new customers regularly. Think how easy it would be to send a holiday greeting to all of your customers at once! I know many businesses like to use paper cards and hand-written letters for a personal touch. By all means, do that if you're so inclined, but if you're trying to save time and money, a well-designed and well-written email will be almost as effective. And save trees.

My main philosophy on business data and all data really is enter it ONCE, in one place. There are so many headaches caused because you need a certain piece of data in a different place, so you go type it again. You're leaving a lot of room for error. Retracing where the error actually happened is a gigantic headache, and not one that you want. If you're struggling with this concept, you should hire a technology specialist to make sure you're using your databases correctly. It's well-worth your money and their time to set this up correctly from the beginning.

Next, automate your billing. In this current marketplace, you have no excuse to be hand-creating and sending invoices through the mail and waiting to receive a check back as payment. If you're not set up to automatically bill your clients, you're missing out. Yes, there are transaction fees. But the less cash you have tied up in your accounts receivable, the more solid your business is. Ideally, you have people's billing information up front. Then your billing system automatically generates an invoice and sends it to them to collect an automatic payment from their card. Setting your billing up to run automatically really saves you time on your bookkeeping it's very easy to synchronize with your accounting software. And when someone doesn't pay right away, you have automatic reminders set up for them.
If there is anything else you find yourself doing over and over, look for ways to automate and systematize it. Again, I realize not everything can be done on a computer, but if you're repeatedly doing the same tasks, perhaps a part

of that process can be automated. At the very least, review how you're doing it each time to see if there's a more efficient way.

Your Health

Systematize your health? No, really, it's possible. These things are going to help you feel and look your best.

We all know we need to be more active. And routinely active. Schedule it to automatically happen. I love fitness trackers for accountability. Set up a reminder to sync your tracker every day. It keeps you more aware of your current status if you look at it every single day. Actually, scheduling your fitness into your calendar is an effective system too. You still have to DO it, but you'll have reminders to get out of your chair more often if you've got a system and a schedule to follow. Build it into your morning routine, and you have a winning formula.

Systematize your eating. Why? Because skipping meals when you're too busy isn't healthy. Not only do you have a growling stomach and potentially bad breath, you'll be low on brain power and your mood will suffer. Yes, "hangry" is a very real thing. Low blood sugar from not eating truly causes your creativity and critical thinking skills to decline because your brain is focused more on meeting it's physiological needs instead of helping you with your projects. Planning your meals is a great strategy for systematizing your eating. It also saves you time and money overall because you won't be eating out, wasting rotten produce from the fridge, or binge eating the bag of chips from the pantry because there's nothing else to eat for dinner.

If you want to stop getting frequent illnesses and create resilient health to bounce back faster when you do catch a bug, take care of your diet and exercise regularly. Prevention is the best medicine, and it is truly the best way to manage your health without chemicals and doctor visits.

Finances

Getting your finances into a system is going to make your life and your book-keeper's so much easier. There are so many ways to turn all aspects of your money-life into systems, in fact, that I can't even cover them all here. I just want to touch on the basics for now.

Automate your savings. This should be your number one priority! You don't have to think about transferring that money over or making a deposit. It just happens. One of my secret methods personally is to have my emergency fund sitting at a bank that I can't physically visit, it's an online bank. I can transfer the money between my banks, but it takes a couple of days. So, using the emergency fund is a conscious choice, not just a quick-and-easy withdrawal. All of the online banking institutions will accept electronic transfers as deposits. Set your deposits up as a direct deposit from your paycheck, did you know you can have that direct deposit split multiple ways? Or as a recurring electronic bill-pay to your savings account. You'll thank me later when you have to use some of that money.

Systematize your debt repayments. In fact, don't just create a system, put that on autopilot. Schedule your payments to come out automatically. Don't think about having to manually pay bills again. Pay your debts off so you can put the money where you want it to go, comfortably. If you've not heard of the debt snowball, Google it. There are free worksheets you can download that walk you through how to get your debts paid faster. It's a great technique.

Get covered and know your insurance needs. Here's another place to automatically pay a bill. But don't skimp and cut this out. Insurance is a pain and can feel like a waste to have. But some kinds are required by law, and let me tell you, if you ever need to use your insurance, you'll be so grateful that you have it.

If you're looking for a pre-designed system for your financial life, I have an e-book for that. It's available on my website www.TheJessicaHansen.com, and it's called Sparkling Finances. I detail my personal secret systems for managing my finances in it.

Hire the help you need. Hire the accountant, bookkeeper, financial planner, and tax-preparer. You aren't specialized and up-to-date on all of the industry trends, laws, and regulations. They know what they're doing and use their knowledge. A solid financial planner will make you more money than you ever pay them, and you can't go wrong hiring a good one. But do your research any time you're hiring someone. Check their references. It's worth the time you have to put into it.

But most importantly - simplify your finances! Put everything on autopilot. Stop spending hours each month paying your bills and reconciling your checkbook. Create a budget and stick to it. You'll feel so much relief to have your finances under control and creating these easy systems will help you sleep at night.

Spiritual Life

What in the world can I mean with a spiritual system? Simply put - add your practices into your daily and weekly routines. Schedule these activities into your calendar and make them a priority. Engage in your activities regularly. Pray, meditate, read scriptures, go outside, do the moon phase rituals - whichever practices you personally use. This will keep you grounded and relieve stress. Admit it, you can use some stress-relief. This part of your routine doesn't have to take over your life. It can be a few minutes a day that you sit in silence and allow your thoughts to clear. But schedule the time into your calendar. And then do it.

Any spiritual practice that you engage in will give you the peace you need. Fill your bucket because you'll be mentally stronger when a disaster happens.

Self-Care

Finally, take care of you. Not just when you get around to it. Actually, make yourself a priority. Check in with yourself regularly and see what you need, and make sure you have your needs met. Eat your meals. Get enough sleep. Exercise. Get a massage. Do what you need to do, scheduled into your calendar as part of your routine.

Take breaks! You can't be "on" 100% of the time. Build down-time into your day. Scheduling yourself for every second isn't sustainable and you'll run yourself ragged.

I have an e-Book about self-care - you should go check out on my website www.TheJessicaHansen.com. It's called Radiant Self. There's a really neat system outlined for you in it.

The three things you need to do

SEVEN

The three things you need to do...

Be Organized.

To have a resilient system, you've got to be organized. Organized time, organized space, organized process. Don't worry it's easier than it sounds. If you're not in the habit of staying organized, let me explain why you want to take steps towards being more organized in your life and business.

When you're wasting time because you're looking for things you know you have, you will wish you were more organized. Spending all that time searching around in and on and under everything isn't practical.

How long does it take you to dig through your kitchen junk drawer to find the best permanent marker and how many did you open up and look at before you found the good one? I know you've been here. Relax, we all have. Even me. The problem is even worse if you have younger people than yourself living in your house with you. Pictures of items in the drawer in the right places helps with those who can't read, or who never seem to remember where things go. If everyone around you can read, a label maker is really going to be your best friend.

Oh, and re-buying things because they're lost, that's another huge waste of money from your pocket. You could be investing that money into yourself and your business, instead of replacing things all the time. Let's not forget the gas you had to use to drive yourself there. And the time you spent. How many times have you stopped at Dollar Tree to buy new scissors because the last 10 pairs you had all walked away?

Now, the organized PROCESS, don't be afraid of it. The basic concept you need to remember is that doing things in the right order keeps you from re-doing, un-doing, and half-doing. If you take a few minutes to think through the steps you're going to take to accomplish something, you will save yourself time, energy, and frustration.

Have you built a Lego set? Boy is it frustrating to find that you didn't follow the steps exactly when 4 pages later it's not going together. If you were 7 years old, you'd probably break down and cry. OK, well, that's probably what I would have done when I was 7. But there's a reason why the steps are done in a certain order, right? Because that's the most efficient way to do it.

To find out if what you're trying to create a process for you could use a tool such as a "spaghetti diagram." To do this, you'll sketch out your space, and each time you have to walk to another location to do a step of the process you'll draw a line from your starting point to your stopping point. At the end of your process, you might see that you went back and forth 8 times in your kitchen just to make dinner. You might review what you did at each stop and see if you can rearrange your cabinets to fit your process better. Or not, but if you want to save time and make your cooking time as easy as it can be, this is a good place to start. But really, you can use this tool for any activity you do.

Be Documented.

t does sometimes seem in this day and age of saving trees that writing down a process to follow is a bit of a waste of paper. I would argue though, that each time you write your process down, you're making it better. Why?

Writing it down helps you think it through. You actually have to sort out your thoughts about what you're doing in what order when you're writing it down instead of just doing something. There's something to writing things down that adds accountability too. I don't know why that's true, but somehow, when you write it just becomes real, right?

For visual learners you'll see the steps and the check-marks showing you're done! That's motivation in action for working through a tough task. Getting to see a tangible result, especially when you're working on a more invisible project, really helps you to keep going.

For kinesthetic learners the actual writing and tapping your pen on each step as you do them - or crossing them off is gratifying. Think of all of the checkmarks you'll be drawing and the steps you're writing on the page! That's taking some action, right there!

Writing a system down communicates it to others so you can delegate! And it communicates it to yourself, so you'll never question if you forgot to do something. Especially for those processes you don't do often, or something you're trying to implement that's new to you.

When you go to delegate, there's no question of what you said to do when you write it down. Unless you lose the piece of paper... but we're going to pretend that won't happen, because now you're organized. You'll never have to deal with people "not hearing" what you said or asking over and over again what is the next thing to do.

The receiver of your instructions or process can come back to the instructions later and ask clarifying questions ahead of time if there is something not explained in enough detail. This is always good practice for you to go over too, because sometimes as you're going back over the process you'll realize there are things you can improve about what you designed.

When you're programming a workflow system, writing it down explains how you automated something, so you don't forget what you programmed. This is VERY important if you're doing work for someone else, or it's a part of your process you want to be able to reuse. Also, when something goes wrong, you'll know where to start looking for the problem. How many passwords have you forgotten in your life? So, what makes you think you'll remember the exact steps in your workflow? Exactly, three weeks from now, you'll have to go back and dig around to remember what you did and where.

Be Automatic.

A resilient system is as automatic as possible. Not necessarily all automated. But automatically triggered. Phone reminders, things put away into the right place, where you'll need the item next time, or even setting out your materials for the next day before you end work today.

The goal is to have no thinking about what or how to do things in the moment. If you're running low on brain power because you're tired or something traumatic happens in your life, you'll be grateful that you don't have to think about what you need to do, where to do it, and when to get it done.

If you're running automatically, you can't get interrupted in the middle by your kids and forget where you stopped, because it's easy to see what you need to do next.

You can't run out of time, because you've planned for all the time you need, and know when everything needs to be done AND how long it's going to take.

You won't be late with a project, to an appointment, or filing your taxes. When you have things systematized, you'll be running everything in small bites, and you won't have the big bad boulder weighing you down.

When you have a resilient system, there's No thinking about WHEN to do things, that's already been decided. Whether you're doing the tasks yourself, or you're delegating them to another person or the computer, tasks are automatically routed based on the assignments you made. You don't have to refer back to what the directions were. Everything is already laid out for you, step by step, with a timeline, and task ownership.

Another way you can automate when you do certain tasks is by using a social media scheduler and an email autoresponder. Emails and posts are automatically sent/posted without you having to log in and do anything. Go to the beach. They'll still go out when you told them to.

If you can have things happen without you touching them, there's no manual labor from you! This is the absolute Bluest-Sky Possibility. If you're thinking through your tasks and are able to automate them (or hire someone to automate them), You can actually take time off for you. There's no more 70-hour work-weeks. Relax. You can breathe again

You can spend time on creating the relationships and content rather than keeping your business going. Go back to being the face of your business. Stop manually running your business operations by the seat of your pants. Make your time matter, and you'll create the massive impact you started out to have.

How to actually create a system.

EIGHT

How to actually create a system.

Alright! Now that you have the background behind what systems are, why you need them, and what they can do for you - it's time to actually create them.

 Don't be afraid.

It's going to be easier than you think.

But give yourself a break too, if you don't get it right away, come back and try again. There is a learning curve when you try something new - always. Recognize that with your new systems and know that you'll be moving forward fast before you even realize you're doing it.

Step 1 - Define the problem

There is really one main goal for everything you're doing in each aspect of your life. Don't mix and match your goals. You end up not doing when you're trying to accomplish conflicting or misaligned goals because you'll always be trying to decide which is more important. When you're stuck not doing anything because you're not making a decision, it's called decision paralysis. My oldest son fell into this trap when deciding what to do after high school - college, work, military, or trade school. He was trying to make everyone happy, and so he couldn't decide what to do and ended up really unhappy himself instead.

Don't fall into that trap, and make sure you're clearly defining what the problem is that you're trying to solve.

My best advice here, when you're trying to decide what problem you're going to tackle, start with small to medium sized problems. If you're not even sure where you COULD start - try the brain-dump trick. Just write all of the problems down that you want to solve, in any order, any problem the comes to mind. Once they're all written down, circle what you're going to work on first. But don't lose the paper you wrote them on. You can come back here when you've solved the first problem and review the list to jog your memory on what you want to solve next.

For this first step, don't think about HOW you're going to solve the problem, only think about WHAT you want to solve. It sounds really basic, but this is really a stumbling block for so many people. Keep in mind here that there are an infinite number of hows, but there's only one what. And the truth here is you probably don't immediately have the answer to how you're going to solve it anyway, so that's not a reason not to know what you want to solve. How comes later.

OK, your decision and analysis paralysis end here. Decide on what you're doing for this small piece of your life. Use a decision tree that we talked about back before to get as close as you can to a solution. You may not get all the way to the final answer. Sometimes you have to take a leap of faith and just choose an action step. The only true wrong answer in life OR business is NO ACTION AT ALL. You can always change your direction later if the results are not achieving the goal you set.

Remember that big problems are often a collection of smaller problems. Break them down into small pieces and solve each one separately. They will end up fitting together. Eat the elephant. Put together the puzzle. One small piece at a time. Don't tackle the biggest thing on your list first.

Step 2 - Define your constraints

This might seem a little strange to say, but even when the sky's the limit, you're working within a set of constraints. What's a constraint? Think of it as the fenced yard. You can basically do anything you want as long as you don't leave the safety of your backyard.

Here's a list of questions to get you thinking about what your particular set of constraints are. Just be cognizant that you are the one putting the limits on yourself. No one else is limiting you here, it's all up to you.

a.   Are you investing money into a solution? How much?

b.   Do you have a limited amount of a particular resource to get this done? (time, space, materials)

c.   How much knowledge do you already have on what you need to do, and can you afford to spend the time to learn more about potential solutions?

d.   Is this something you need to hire out because there is a specialization required to finish the job? Or maybe for a piece of the solution but not the entire strategy?

e.   Is there a particular software you can or can't use - or that doesn't work on your computer?

f.   Any other restrictions on the solution?

Let me tell you a story. I once helped a photographer put together her CRM system. She had bought the software because someone had recommended it to her but had never used it because she became overwhelmed at the thought of programming it. I had to ask a lot of questions to determine the actual constraints of what she was trying to do with her business and client follow up. But when we were done, she had a full set of workflows for 4 types of photoshoots and a full annual follow-up email sequence set-up to go out automatically.

Step 3 - Do the research

This is going back a little bit to the constraints you just brainstormed through. Chances are, to design the system to solve the problem you've identified as being your current focus, you'll be doing some research. Knowledge is power. Don't let what you don't know stop you. Google is your friend. You can find all kinds of other ways people have solved a similar problem to yours, and there will be blog posts about what they did indexed by all of the major search engines. Big hint here: don't look at only one of the solutions you find. Read a few different ways of designing the system that seem to fit for you, and then use the best parts of all of them. They will each have different strengths.

Occasionally, you'll get stuck with how to create a system. When you do, Enlist the help of an expert. People like me exist for a reason!

Do restrict the time you spend on the research stage, though. Make sure you have a definite time limit for how long you're going to be searching for an answer. Don't get sucked into the rabbit hole of Pinterest. AWESOME ideas. Most are not related to the actual problem we need to solve. Oh, hey, maybe I'll make THAT for dinner tonight. THAT's a great outfit! Whoa. What were we talking about again?

Step 4 - Make a plan

Key point - NOTHING is set in stone. Don't get stuck on thinking you can't change what you're doing later, even after you've started. Some progress in the right direction and then tweaking the plan is better than never starting at all! DO NOT allow yourself to think that you have to have everything perfectly detailed before you start. Scribble the steps down on a napkin with a crayon while you're at the park with the kids and the baby is sleeping. It doesn't have to have a specific format.

BUT YOU MUST WRITE IT OUT. No, you won't remember next week what you decided to do. I know you enough to know that you have a ton of things going on, and you'll come back later and have to reinvent the wheel again or at least put the wheel back on! Therefore, wasting time. And hey, if you did write it on a napkin with a crayon - snap a picture of that napkin before you use it to clean up the baby's chin.

Making a plan is another place an expert can help you if you're stuck. Using an expert to see a new angle on the solution gives you new options. Expert planners generally have seen how other people do similar things and may be able to sniff out what you're missing. Remember here that you missed it NOT because you're not capable, but because you simply lack the experience and it's okay.

The last step of your plan is to decide how often you're going to review the system to see if it's working for you and make tweaks if necessary. Let's use my own Morning routine as an example here - I can't tell you how often I am changing up what I have in my routine and what I cut out.

It changes monthly, as my business changes, or my family is taking on different activities, or I decide to give a different fitness program a try. Remember how I said it was OK to change what you're doing? That's why you're building in a review here. You're going to come back to it as often as you need to and change what's not working. You'll be able to recognize it. Even if you think everything is OK, review it at your interval anyway. Maybe you dropped a step without realizing it, and as it turns out that step was overkill and not necessary anyway. Cross it out! Clear the clutter of your system. Make sure you touch it and tell it thank you for existing before you release it. It might get offended if you cross it out without acknowledging it's presence.

Step 5 - Do it

Work through the plan once. USE what steps you wrote down for reference. Make some notes about what felt good or not when you hit your first review interval. Maybe that's the end of the first day or the first week. It may be longer if the system is around something you have to do monthly or annually.

Don't change it up in the first round, because this is how you got so stuck. You decided what you're doing, so unless you hit a hard stop, keep going exactly how you wrote it out. Yes, it might be foreign. Yes, it might be tough to get through. Jot notes down in those rough patches, but don't stop unless you have to. There IS a difference between HAVING TO and choosing to.

Lastly, review the outcome constantly at intervals over a long period of time. You already decided your review intervals in step 4 when you made your plan, so stick to it. This review step is extremely important because if you don't review what you're doing, you're not improving anything in your life, since there's never a measurement of any progress or not.

Schedule the reviews to be automatic. Phone pop up reminders are a good idea. Schedule them for a time when you know you won't be engaged in other important tasks that will delay your review. It can be a 5-minute reflection. Maybe you find when the pop up happens, you realize you quit doing the morning routine on Wednesday last week. Why did you get derailed? What about it felt overwhelming?

This practice of reviewing what's going on at intervals in your life is a great way to get to know YOU.

The more you know about yourself and what's making YOU tick, the easier it will be to create the systems in your life.

What trips you up every time?
Are you triggered by too many phone pop-up reminders?
Does a list of 30 tasks make you run the other way?

Great! Now you know, so we can come up with a different solution! Celebrate that. And realize how much valuable information you just gained from that quick review of your process!

Don't stop here. Get more resources and

continue your resilient journey

www.TheJessicaHansen.com.

About the Author – Jessica Hansen

I am an overcomer.

My journey REALLY started as a teenager. I suffered some serious setbacks. I lost friends. I lost family. Lost out on a lot of fun. Lost myself. I gained a son.

But the trials didn't end. I gained a severe case of depression, drug and alcohol problems, leaving everything I knew behind to move across the country, counseling, medication, homelessness, domestic violence, welfare, bankruptcy, single parenting. And, I gained another son, a college education, a fantastic corporate job, a new appreciation of the power of God, a wonderful husband, and finally two more children.

My mantra through it all: "I can do anything I decide to do."

No matter what's going on in the background. Even when it's hard.

I didn't give up.

What kept me afloat in all of this?
A resilient mindset.

Massive amounts of creativity.

Looking at the bigger picture.

A system for everything.

What I did was create systems to deal with all of the day-to-day things. While my corporate job educated me. We studied all of the LEAN principles, read the Toyota Way, learned about Six-Sigma, and created hundreds of Continuous Improvement ideas - and then implemented them. I learned that systems work.

I studied systems and created processes in all areas of my life. When I left my corporate job on maternity leave with my third son (and subsequently was laid off), I went process-crazy at home, creating a killer chore chart for my kids, time-management schemes, meal planning, and everything else. (I ALMOST labeled all of my kitchen cabinets and drawers to make sure things were always put back where they belonged.)

I created systems that brought me from $50,000 in debt up to a net worth over a million. I created a life for me and my family based on what I learned on the job. And now, I am sharing it with you.

Because it works.
Now, I help women like you to create the freedom they desire.

Because you want to travel.

Because you want to say "YES" when opportunity appears.

Because you want to do what you want, when you want it, no restrictions.

You want to be free.

That's exactly what these core systems will do for you. When you're ready to stop doing all.the.things, and keep your business GROWING, efficient systems are the key.

Let's do this. www.TheJessicaHansen.com

Acknowledgements

Thank you, Erica for making this all possible. You pulled me from my invisibility cloak, one thread at a time, and I owe you so much more than just a thank you.

Thank you to my family for supporting me, even when you had no idea what I was up to.

Thank you to all of the amazing women I have met along my journey, you are too numerous to name, but I am inspired by you, and know that I would not be here today making a difference if I had not had you telling me to keep going.